FAT GIRL FORMS

STEPHANIE ROGERS

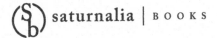

saturnalia | BOOKS

Distributed by Independent Publishers Group
Chicago

Saturnalia Books
105 Woodside Rd.
Ardmore, PA 19003
info@saturnaliabooks.com

ISBN: 978-1-947817-32-6 (print), 978-1-947817-33-3 (ebook)
Library of Congress Control Number: 2021938915

Cover art and book design by Robin Vuchnich

Distributed by:
Independent Publishing Group
814 N. Franklin St.
Chicago, IL 60610
800-888-4741

I'd like to thank the Editors of the following journals in which several poems in this collection have previously appeared, sometimes in earlier versions:

Another Chicago Magazine: "Fat Girl Quatern"

Broadsided Press: "Fat Girl Triolet"

Copper Nickel: "Fat Girl Cascade"; "Fat Girl Ghazal"

CutBank Literary Journal: "Fat Girl Lira"; "Fat Girl Terzanelle"

DIAGRAM: "Fat Girl Sestina"; "Fat Girl Terza Rima"

Georgia Review: "Fat Girl Crown"

The Pinch: "Fat Girl Penta Rima"

Poetry Northwest: "Fat Girl Duo-Rhyme"; "Fat Girl Ballade"

Rattle: "Fat Girl Trilonnet"

Shenandoah: "Fat Girl LaCharta"; "Fat Girl Trenta-Sei"

Tin House: "Fat Girl Triumphal Ode"

Western Humanities Review: "Fat Girl Memento"

I'm grateful for the guidance of Sandra Beasley, Kathleen Ossip, Lynn Melnick, Maggie Smith, Jenn Givhan, Timothy Liu, and Christopher Salerno. I'm thankful for the friendship of Amber Leab, Kerri French, Matt Feltman, and Christopher Culwell. I'm especially appreciative of Henry Israeli and everyone at Saturnalia Books for believing in my work. And thank you to Robin Vuchnich for designing the wonderful cover. I'd also like to thank the two teachers who taught me how to write in form, Andrew Hudgins and Joanie Mackowski. Immense gratitude to my family for their love and encouragement: Rhonda Rogers, Heather McKanna, Ian Rogers, Sophia McKanna, Chloe McKanna, and Penelope McKanna. And to my husband, Josh Ralske, for his friendship, unwavering support, and for loving my fat ass without judgment.

CONTENTS

ONE

TWO

THREE

Without fat girls, there would be no protests.

—Ann Coulter, Twitter 2016

... And the moon,
under its dark hood,
falls out of the sky each night,
with its hungry red mouth
to suck at my scars.

—Anne Sexton, from "As It Was Written"

ONE

::

FAT GIRL RONDELET

       I strut the street
with this fat body. Swaying my hips,
       I strut the street
and swirl. Fat body greets the heat
on summer days. Fat body flips
the bird. Along the late-night strip,
       I strut the street.

FAT GIRL TRIOLET

       The moon doesn't make a single sound
though the rain starts up outside. I hear it
       rattling my windows as the light bends,
but the moon doesn't make a single sound.
       I'm just as fat as she is up there, round
as raindrops splattering the ground. I fear it.
       The moon doesn't make a single sound
though the rain starts up outside. I hear it.

FAT GIRL VILLANELLE #1

I stare at my body in a photograph
where all my friends surround me, smiling.
But I don't recognize that girl, that laugh

around her eyes and the crinkled grin. A brass
doorknob reflects the spark of her teeth.
I stare at her body in a photograph

and see the light streaking across her calf,
her bare thighs. I peer, close up, and breathe.
I don't recognize that girl. That laugh

gets me, how her hair flows down her back,
unleashed. I want to touch her, extend my reach,
not stare at her body in a photograph

or to watch her without knowing her, to crack
a smile even now, to avoid disrupting
what I don't recognize. That girl, laughing,

who is she? I want to own her body, to lift
her from the room. I want to end the grief
of staring at that body in a photograph
when I don't recognize that girl, that laugh.

FAT GIRL ALOUETTE

I want the way birds
want, to soar like words
escaping a lost lover's
tongue saying, *come back,*
come back. How wings flap
through air. How I take cover

inside my blue heart,
ignoring the part
where it flutters, its soft beat
unnerving my chest
like those birds, their nest
withered by some storm I eat

with my whole body—
wait. Now I'm ready
for rain ticking against me,
for rain. Where those birds
go, I go, absurd
at rest, weighing down the trees.

FAT GIRL OVILLEJO

Each day, I wake to ready
      my body
            to devour the sun's heat,
    to eat
the thick and dripping light.
      The night
            swells around me, scares
the day, so I prepare
            my body to eat the night.

FAT GIRL RONDEAU

The fat girl knows when you notice her, resigned
to her body. The fat girl knows the longing kind
of look, never toward her. Whenever your gaze
touches her face, you look away, which says:

I'm ashamed for you. I wonder if you could find
your heart if it were shoved beneath your eyes,
resting in her palm, a wet peeled plum, amazed
the fat girl knows

your body looks like hers inside. But your mind
won't hear it. You think she wants you, pines
for you, needs your hands on her, unfazed
by your disgust. Bitch, please. Watch the way
her eyes roll into her skull when you walk by.
The fat girl knows.

FAT GIRL KYRIELLE SONNET

I eat my fingernails. I eat
            the scraps leftover from the meat,
the barbecue. I bite into
            a tulip twirling through the blue

night air where I absorb the silk
            of it. My teeth swallow the milk
the stars rain down and then I chew
            a tulip twirling through the blue

again. I eat the purple weeds
            that dance along the highway, seeds
of dandelions springing through
            a tulip twirling through the blue.

I eat my fingernails. I eat,
            a tulip twirling through the blue.

FAT GIRL BLUES SONNET

I wonder how it feels to move my body.
I wonder how to feel about my body
when it moves without me. I'm not ready

to remember how to move the way the thin
remember how to move. The way the thin
people surround me, I can't even begin

to fit in. The thin girls hang against the walls.
The thin girls fit in, hanging against the walls
like wallflowers, the decorated halls

of a high school prom, and when they move,
the high school prom lights blink and move
around the room. I've always wanted to love

my body, but here's the thing about it, reader:
Maybe thin girls can't love their bodies, either.

FAT GIRL HAIKU

Sun pinches eyes closed.
I move within her body,

wishing it were mine.

FAT GIRL PANTOUM

Who sweats the most in eighty-five degrees?
This girl—shit—when I'm walking to the train
or when I wake, like how the backs of my knees
        go all damp in the dark, along with my brain.

        This girl—shit—when I'm walking to the train,
I carry a wad of paper towels in my hand.
I go all damp in the dark and somehow my brain
        feels like I tried to claw it out last night. And

        I carry a wad of paper towels in my hand
to wipe myself down while people watch. My face
looks like I tried to claw it off last night. And
        redness, redness flashes all over the place.

        I wipe myself down while people watch my face
going all wow against the backdrop of the sun:
redness, redness flashes all over the place.
        When she burns me up like this, it's like a gun

going all wow against the backdrop of the sun.

And when I wake, the backs of my knees

burn me up. Like this—just like a gun—

I sweat the most in eighty-five degrees.

FAT GIRL MEMENTO

The anniversary of fat

        arrives today! The scale

hates you

as much as last year's scale. Your hats

        don't even fit, you whale.

You grew!

FAT GIRL ACROSTIC

Fuck you, doctor. No, I don't care
about my body mass index score, that outdated

test meant to say:
Get your fat ass up and exercise.

I'm off my fat ass, exercising every day. So
reach into your hat where you
lost my good-ass blood work, my good-
ass cheekbones lookin' all fly in the face of your
contempt. Do you know what it feels like when you
roam your eyes up and down my body,
ogling my fat tits, my
stretch marks on my naked upper arms?
Take a big shit on your advice and heft me up.
In my dreams, I'm no bigger than your bullshit
cock, lonely as the fat girls under fluorescent lights.

FAT GIRL RISPETTO

Daytime takes a seat and night
        stands. I'm outside watching myself,
my body's looming dark where light
                casts my shadow. The filth

on the ground—gum stuck to the sidewalk,
        initials carved in concrete—talks
beside the outline of my body.
        I crouch to touch it, fattening the copy.

FAT GIRL BALLADE

I ask for my seat-belt extender on the plane.

       The flight attendant smirks as she hands it over

though I decide to smile, avoiding a scene

       I've rehearsed a hundred times. Under the cover

of her thin body, she watches me—whatever—

       while I buckle myself into the smallest seat

I've felt. My body overflows. My neighbor

       rolls her eyes, so I roll mine back, then eat

a snack before we take off (because I'm crazed

       and need to pop my Xanax and food together).

I look to make sure no one watches. My brain

       spins when I hear the engine. She towers

over me. *Ma'am, are you okay?* as the plane

       takes off, my hands clutching the armrest. *Great!*

I yell back and ignore the way she hovers,

       rolls her eyes. But I roll mine back then eat

her face off in my mind, try to lick the rain-

      drops off the window next to me—my lover

suddenly—and then a drugged-up grin

      creeps around my mouth. (Xanax, the bringer

of peace, the bringer of song, the harbinger

      of spring!) And then I forget I'm the fat

girl on the plane, the fattest girl no longer!

      I roll my eyes. I roll them back while eating

the way the people think I eat—*to devour*.

      "to eat up greedily." The attendant darts

away from me but peeks back to discover

      I'm rolling. My eyes roll back again. I eat!

FAT GIRL MONOTETRA

I wake, listening to the leaves

    move the trees, and all the graves

        come back to me, and all the grief

            falls over me, falls over me,

like how my father fell asleep

    in blood. He always had a grip

        on my body. Somehow, I keep

            hearing the trees, hearing the trees

sway outside my window, my fat

    knees touching, my hair spread out

        across my pillow. I know what

            happens to that, happens to that

kind of woman, the kind who stays

    awake for it, who always craves

        a way to end what people say

            about her face, about her face:

You're beautiful (never about

    her body). I wonder out loud

        to my hands: Why aren't you proud

           and not the sad, and not the sad

woman who listens to the leaves

    move the trees, imagining ways

        to disappear her body? Please

           come back to me, come back to me.

FAT GIRL QUATERN

Because no one sees me, I go
to work high. I go there naked.
I go nowhere and upward all
at once. I take my hands and twist

a joint. I grip all my fat rolls
because no one sees me. I go
huge! I stand next to a flower
pot and squat to piss and no one

notices—I'm invisible
to you and you and you and just
because no one sees me I go
along with it. The sky turns black

with it. The trees kill leaves for it.
My nails rip my eyes with it, rip
my tongue. I'm so clawed and I'm stoned.
Because no one sees me, I go.

TWO

::

FAT GIRL PENTA RIMA

The thing is—are we greedy
to want? Because I'm fat,
     I hide inside an ocean
of guilt, my body a flat
        note in a pretty

     melody. The motion
of my body chases away
     the bystanders who watch
but have nothing to say
     about their devotion

     to my body. I light a match
for them when I feel alone
     and blow it out like a storm
that threatens the buried bones
     in a shallow patch

of grass where dogs still worm

their prizes into the earth.

      I mean to say I'm sorry

about how my self-worth

           depends on warm

         bones clicking a flurry

against me, electrified

    but charred the way the needy

breathe. If I want to hide

          forever, let me.

FAT GIRL SPLIT COUPLETS

        You make me pick the taste buds off my tongue
and eat my lungs,
           grab a knife and slice my body open,
take the ripened
           blood vessels and suck the red and suck
the yellow muck
        that oozes toward my face. You make me lick
the way the sick
          inhale their oxygen, to need it not to
die. Like you
          I grew, so tell me why you hate my body
like it's some shoddy
          car I built so wrong the car won't start
and every part
        of the engine grinds its gears? You tell me that
I'm so fat
          I can't really object to what you say.
So I stay.

FAT GIRL CAVATINA

I try on a pair of shorts from last year's closet.
      What the fuck—
I can't button them up, zip them even. I'm shit
      out of luck

like my father used to say: *You're shit out of luck.*
      He was right
much of the time but never about my body
      which he said

would always stay athletic, evenly muscled.
      I got fat
before he died and fatter after. What do you
      think of that

bullshit? And yes I'm talking to you, reader.
Do you want to weigh in? (I'll ask again later.)

FAT GIRL TRILONNET

All the stars go down and I
lie on my back in the yard watching
the light dimming, hearing the break

of branches, of leaves sweeping as eyes
search the black, insects calling,
listening to the swirling lake

where frogs go operatic-like
and my body croons along, catching
itself. Tell me what I can take

away from this forgetting, why
I overlook my body, latching
onto the blues the nighttime makes,

how I avoid the light, my past,
and disappear into the grass.

FAT GIRL ABECEDARIAN

                          All my life I've hated my

body. Even thin, I hated my body enough to

                          carve into the skin of it,

dance the blade over it

                          every day

for a year, cover the scars, which

               grew soft and faint, pencil lines drawn on paper,

hardly noticeable after

                   I pressed a tissue against them,

just enough peroxide to clot them, the

                 kitchen scissors placed back in the drawer

lying sideways with

          my body remembered there, crisscrosses gleaming clean

next to the forks, the spoons

                on top of the butter knives, too dull to

push against me, too

        quiet to make my face flinch with the slice of it, no tears

raining down with it. How do I make

sense of it when I never

told anyone till now? Now my fat body

      understands how to punish itself in private, scars less

visible now than

                 when I made them then,

x-ray stills of raised light bouncing off my forearms,

        yellow turned to white. And still I trace the fat

zigzags across me, searching for signs of my body.

FAT GIRL SESTINA

Won't someone touch me again? I've reached out
  a hundred times. I've touched myself hard
and slow, running my fingertips over, under
  the sheets where a man's hands lived once,
his teeth ripping at the seams of my body,
   his teeth dull and sharp against the last

place a man touched me. The thing is last
  night, I dreamed again how to figure out
the way to love my body. I touched my body
  in the dream where a man's tongue hardened
against me, wet as the peeled apple once
   pressed to my lips by another man under

the cover of moonlight. It was pretty under
        there, yellow reflected off the car hood, last
kiss under trees that held the leaves I once
        jumped through as a child, climbed out
from beneath, brushing them off my hard
        kneecaps, my hands, my breasts. My body

doesn't understand how so many bodies
        come off beautiful in the magazines under
their softened lights when my body hardly
        even notices itself in sunlight. My last
therapist told me to stop, to listen, to get out
        of my own head about my body. Then once

he said I should slink down to my knees, once

    I figured out who my god was, and pray my body

back to thin again. I dropped him, got out

        fast from underneath, crawled under

my own skin and disappeared like last

        night's darkness. I've grown numb to hard

knocks, the insults. Body—fat, thick—hardly

        pays attention anymore. But once, just once,

a man kissed the flesh off my body, his last

        touch so soft I felt the wind against it, body

swimming through it, not once going under.

        Won't someone touch me again? Get me out

of here? I'll hold my body's hard fat heart out

        for one last time, no longer a thing kept

under wraps. Whoever you are, take it.

FAT GIRL CINQUAINS

I lie
              against the grass
blades in the yard knowing
       you'll never touch my fat body
again.

I left
             before you left,
my body way out from
       under you, bending, a flower
drooping.

How does
             a body move
freely when a body
       listens to those who hate the way
it moves?

Body:

                    ignored. Body:

disgusting. Fat body

    you're ashamed to touch in public.

Hear me.

The clouds

                    drift overhead

and I remember why

    I loved you before. You called me

pretty.

FAT GIRL RUBLIW

Oh fat

girl in the rat

race, I want to chat

about the way you sometimes bat

your lashes at the men who like your cat

eyes but not your fat thighs, your brat-

ass snipes, your matte

lipstick, the tat

on your lat

so let's

make a bet:

the solitary wet

mouth you'll catch against the net

of you will bite your tongue, will rip the jet

winds from your hair. Fat girl, you met

some lips and rushed to set

a fire. Yet

he pet

another—

how he placed her

hands against the blur

of your fattening face like the whir

of fan blades singing acoustic, spewing the air

toward you. He somehow knew for sure

you'd fail again to lure

a man, discover

a lover.

FAT GIRL ITALIAN SONNET

The tulip droops its blue head to the ground,

faces my hands as I press them against the dirt

        so softly I feel the gravel as I put

my fingers in. They hardly make a sound.

Then his words come back to me, the found-

out secret, a thing he couldn't help but blurt

to his friends: *Man, that bitch is fat, that skirt*

        kept riding so far up her ass, the pounds

just jiggling, and me and my bros could see

        her fucking tits all bouncing like a slapped

pig's butt. My friend told me that everyone

        at the party laughed. The tulip holds a bee

in its heart, and I can't help but bend to wrap

        the petals in my palms, whisper: *Eat the sun.*

FAT GIRL TERZA RIMA

       I walk across the vacant street at night,

my arms covered, wrapped around my chest

    like a kind of hiding. I know it's getting late,

      so late I watch the sky turn pink, impressed

by its own sadness. Sometimes I think I want

    to die. But not in this body. Laying me to rest

      in an oversized coffin. This body in the front

of some—what—church? while onlookers look,

    wide eyes destroying everything they meant

      to hide behind them. No one ever took

me this seriously or stuck around long enough

    to get the joke. The joke is I never once spoke

to anyone about my body. Easier to laugh

at the joke of my body with the onlookers

or to think of loving my body, that stiff

smile. That smile? It's the joke too, funnier

than some. But I only want to die some

of the time like when it's night, vacant, lighter

than expected. When the air gets cool, a flame

on the tip of a cigar pressed against my body.

That's how it feels. Even small, I felt the same.

FAT GIRL GHAZAL

At the bar, I ran into a frat boy who called me a fat girl.
He said, "No one wants to sleep with a fucking fat girl."

I opened my thighs, joked with him, "Pretty please?"
Later, I mascara-wrecked my pillow, a crying fat girl.

Once, a homeless man freaked out when I ignored him.
He yelled, "Move, you stupid bitch, you fucking fat girl."

I won't lie. I called my sister while sobbing on the toilet.
She said, "What is *wrong* with people?" I said, "Fat girls?"

My boyfriend says he loves my waves of flab, my breasts.
All his exes: skinny. Is he just pretending to like a fat girl?

Get over yourself, I tell myself in mirrors, in reflections.
Because! I'm tired of playing the funny one, the fat girl.

A driver screamed, "Get your fat ass out of the street."
I looked down, picked up my pace. Ashamed. A fat girl.

I suck in my stomach, pull back my shoulders, envious:
the blondes who ride my block on bikes aren't fat girls.

Some days I accidentally heave my weight in public.
People stare, "Don't sit there. Oh shit—another fat girl."

I'm taught to either love my body or hate it. Love it, hate it.
Even friends think, "Steph, you're pretty! (for a fat girl)."

FAT GIRL VILLANELLE #2

You hate my body, stare at me, astounded

                     that I'd "let it go." When I'm alone

I cradle my body, wrapping my arms around it.

I overhear your insults. Don't worry. They've landed

                     hard against me, my skin as smooth as bone.

But you hate my body, stare at me, astounded

that I don't arrest myself. I hate the sound

                     your eyes make rolling back. What do you gain?

I cradle my body, wrapping my arms around it

like a child holding her favorite doll, her gown

                     cascading to cover her body. Tell me again

how you hate my body. Stare at me, astounded.

I'll still walk the fucking streets, man. I'll announce

                     my presence, my fat ass bending shadows.

I'll cradle my body, wrapping my arms around it

like a prize won at a carnival. I've crowned it

Queen of Fatness, and my hips explode the throne.

        But you hate my body, stare at me, astounded

that I cradle my body, wrapping my arms around it.

FAT GIRL CURTAL SONNET

How much longer does it need to take,

surgeon, for you to look me in the eye,

to pause. I'm not my body or I'm not *just*

my body, thick, my spread-out thighs, the cake-

inhaling monster fat girl of your night-

mares. Look at me. Let's discuss the lust

I feel for your gaze. Yes, surgeon, I desire

too and sleep with all the men I like—

not you. You wonder how this feels? You must,

surgeon. Well, I can't hide my hatred, my

disgust.

FAT GIRL CLANG

I'll take this spark of light ahead

                 and wear it on my face

so people get to see my teeth

                 when I chomp on their bones

which taste like ash, a street shadow

               that—just like light—still roams

across my bulging stomach then

                 leaves without a trace.

FAT GIRL VILLONNET

A stranger follows me down the street at night
      after the party. The dress I wear twirls up
when the wind passes, and I spin to get a grip,
      pressing it against my thighs. The bite

of the cool air makes me shiver in the light
      of a pinked-out bar sign. The man keeps up. I trip.
My heel falls off. I bend to pick it up.
      A stranger follows me down the street. At night

I can hardly see a thing. In the blackness I turn right,
      and that's when I spot another guy who slips
his tongue between his fingers, purses his lips,
      yells into the darkness, "Fat bitch, lose some weight."

Two strangers follow me down the street at night
      joking like they own my body. They move, close up,
yell into the darkness, "Fat bitch, lose some weight."

FAT GIRL LA'TUIN

Stop watching me. Just leave me alone,
I want to scream to match the scowl
　　　　on every boy's face who passes this
fat body, jokes with friends, pokes fun

　　　　like a boy, worst kind of boy, latest one
to ogle my fat body. How
　　　　　　he stares. How I want to know why his
eyes move over me, want that spun-

　　　　around head of his to snap back, run
his eyes along another now
　　　　　　just as slow. I hardly know the kiss
against my fattest parts, so done-

　　　　to-me in secret, so boy-with-gun-
shy hands at first searching the wow
　　　　　　between my thighs. How he whispers, *Please*
don't tell a soul. Fat girl, have fun

with the boys who make you hide in sun
like an insect inside a bow

     tied around your throat. But how they miss
you each time they leave. How they grin

     and won't stop watching. *Leave me alone!*
I want to scream to match the scowl

       on every boy's face who passes this
fat body, jokes with friends. I'm done.

FAT GIRL DUPLEX

I never wanted to be the fat girl.
Everyone in the world pokes fun.

I poke fun like everyone in the world.
I pull my shirt down, hiding my stomach.

My stomach hides inside the shirt I pull down.
I rub baby powder inside my bra.

Baby, my hands smooth powder inside my bra.
No one called me baby for almost ten years.

For ten years I called myself a baby.
I blew kisses to myself in reflections.

I kissed myself in reflections, blew away.
Drunk men in bars won't even look at me.

Look at me trying to fuck drunk men in bars.
I never wanted to be the fat girl.

FAT GIRL RUBAIYAT

Whose fat this is I think I know.

        My body dances along the rows

of people peering who want to hear

        my thighs smacking. I rip my clothes

while twirling by. I disappear

        inside their looks. (The people sneer

when I move past.) I watch them take

        pictures of me, and while they leer

this time I start to curl and snake

        my body to the ground. I shake

in rain—I'm naked now—and weep

        a river into my palms to wake

my hands, my lashes up. The heaps

        of clothes I tore and left to seep

in rainwater dissolve. I leap

        in rainwater. Dissolve. I leap.

FAT GIRL MONCHIELLE

I buy my clothes online.

    Avoid my doctor's face.

Never eat with others.

    Never want to dress this

body for the summer.

I buy my clothes online.

    Don't go to carnivals.

I'm too fat for the rides.

    Ignore disgusted looks

when people whistle by.

I buy my clothes online.

    Never any patterns.

Don't go to the movies.

   The seats won't hold me there.

Look at all the beauties—

when I buy clothes online,

      the women look so thin!

Their skin seems soft as rain.

      The funny thing about it:

my skin feels just the same.

FAT GIRL ROUNDELAY

Just listen to the way my thighs
sweep and listen to the way
I feel, light as a bug that flies
into moonlight. Let me stay
in light along the weeping sky
with clouds so fat I grow afraid

to feel light as a bug that flies
into moonlight. Someone stay
and watch until my body tries
to shed itself, to hold its face
in light along the weeping sky
with clouds so fat I grow afraid

to watch. Until my body tries
to hold itself, to hold its face
reflected in a mirror, eyes
locked on eyes, I'll learn to pray
in light. Along the weeping sky
with clouds so fat I grow afraid

of my reflection in a mirror, eyes

locked on eyes. I'll learn to pray

that way, clutching all my lies

against my chest. I want to sway

in light along the weeping sky

with clouds. So fat, I grow afraid.

THREE

::

FAT GIRL CASCADE

Please don't close your eyes. I want to see

        your eyes, where light reflects me there,

                my body thin, a pin-prick figurine

for once. Hold me for a moment

        in the gleam. Meet my gaze.

                Please don't close your eyes. I want to see

the way my body changes, how it shrinks

        as you move away. Stay far away.

                Your eyes, where light reflects me there,

can hold me all night long but don't come

        close. Just let me watch the way I slink,

                my body thin, a pin-prick figurine.

FAT GIRL PARADELLE

I don't know how to speak about my body anymore.

        My body doesn't know how to speak anymore.

Whenever I bare my body, it rebels against the weather.

        I rebel against my body whenever the weather's bare.

Bare: my body. The weather. I rebel against speaking.

        How don't I know what my body doesn't speak about?

Who can answer me when I go on like this?

        Can someone answer me when I go on like this?

The storm sounds like a crane crashing in the sky.

        A crane crashes in the sky sounding like a storm.

I go on like this, crashing like a storm in someone.

        Like this, a crane answers the sky when I answer.

My body is a storm electrocuting the trespassers.

        Trespassers electrocute the storm of my body.

I don't want you to touch me while I'm still fat.

        I'm still and fat and touched that you don't want me.

My body is a trespasser I don't want to touch.

        Electrocute my still body while I'm the fat storm.

My body rebels like a storm I don't speak about.

       Can someone go on and rebel against the trespassers?

I'm fat as a crane answering the sky: *I don't want touch.*

       The weather of my electrocution crashes me bare.

Like this I go on, crashing into my bare body.

       What don't you want to speak about when touching me?

FAT GIRL TANKA

Cover my body,
fat and naked, with a white
sheet to breathe into
as my lover's crimson tongue
trembles me into a star.

FAT GIRL ONCE

Tell me why you assume I loathe myself
because I'm fat, even though my body

roams in houses meant for goddesses,
a crown on top of my head. I want to flip

you over, slick my fingers along your spine
till you forget to breathe. I know a wealth

of tricks. I sway like leafless trees and dine
on flesh. I lick my bloody lips. I grip

my breasts which won't fit in your bodices
but glitter under touch. Let's grab your rowdy

friends and yank my nighty from the shelf.

FAT GIRL TERZANELLE

Fat girl, get up! It's time to fuck this party,

get out now. The boys all want to screw

your girls. Get up! It's time. Fuck this party

and fuck these boys who only want to do

your girls, not you. Just kidding. They want

to do you too. The boys all want to screw

you secretly. Let's go! Let's pull a stunt

like this: unbutton your shirt, watch them bang

your girls, not you. Just kidding. Boys want

to move against you all close up and hang

like blinking lights that twirl around the trees.

Like this: unbutton your shirt and watch it bang

against their faces, against their muscles, breeze

pushing back their hair. Put on a show

like blinking lights that twirl around the trees.

Flash them your giant tits before you go.

Fat girl, get up! It's time to fuck this party,

pull back your hair. Put on a show,

fat girl. Get up! It's time to fucking party.

FAT GIRL LIRA

Me? I hit so stay
if you want. You can run your hands along my skirt
and I'll kiss you the way
a mother smooches her boy on his head or his wart
even. You're like a wart

to me. I don't like the way
you look at me, you ogle me, make fun of the smart
girls. You're like the filet
I fried to a crisp. Your face? It fell apart
so I ate you after I charred

you like a corpse, okay?
(I tear the gristle from all my meat, imagine the flirt
of bees in the May
weather.) Whether you call me fat or heart-
less is fine. I'm not hurt

by your words but your eyes

that travel up the thick of my calves, ass, the shirt

where my tits display

a FAT AND PROUD logo. You go berserk

for it. You fucking jerk.

FAT GIRL OTTAVA RIMA

I watched Heather give birth three times. I cut
　　　　the umbilical cord twice. Hearing
my sister scream. Screaming at her: *You've got*
　　　　this. I touched each of her babies' tearing
eyes, wiped the gunk from their faces, put
　　　　my hands on her new body. Her baring
teeth, even after the birth, shocked me into
　　　　a smile I hid from her. The way her body grew

from the sleek. The way I always envied her
　　　　body. No one ever asked her what she weighed
even when her stomach ballooned, the blur
　　　　of her face hiding inside a new face
I still knew. People described her kinder
　　　　than me, prettier, not in that *mean* way,
but like I could get there if I tried harder,
　　　　exercised, cared more, ate better. Like Heather.

FAT GIRL TERZA RIMA SONNET

I don't understand a thing. I feel so lost

                in my body, in my mind. The way even

my jaw hurts, clenched, when I think about the cost

of a not-small body no one wants. To believe in

                myself in a world that hates me, the very sight

of me. To believe in my fat face, the beaten

down parts like where my thighs meet, right

                there, almost at the knees. Listen to the sound

they make, the way smooth skin burns in tight

jeans. I keep thinking I've learned by now

                how to live in my body, to forget to care,

to walk without sucking my stomach in, to ground

my brain. I haven't. I don't know how to get there

                or how to breathe while the whole world watches, stares.

FAT GIRL DUO-RHYME

I like stalking the rats that scurry
across my stoop. They're in a hurry
almost every night. And the moon—
I can't stop looking at the moon—
beats the concrete into a room
where rats and I exist: as groom,
as bride. I turn away as one
person turns away from the gloom
of another, wanting only strewn
clothes on the floor, a lover soon
beneath my fat body, my cherry
lips on point, my mouth purring.

FAT GIRL TRENTA-SEI

I don't know what the stars mean. I don't know

why I stand underneath the black and stare

up at the pinprick light. I want so much to glow

in the dark, for everyone to see me, a pair

of fat white thighs blinking in the moonlight

like their own flashing bulbs. I no longer like

why I stand underneath the black and stare

when I'm so lonely the whites of my eyes

brim hot with fire and my dark-brown hair

explodes into a red waterfall. I don't tell lies

like this so often. But a man once took

my body, held it near him while I looked

up at the pinprick light. I wanted so much to glow

like a meteor shooting across the skyscape,

breasts bare, nipples two knotted pink bows

and that man's fingertips swirling my scraped

kneecaps, tender as the rain on my tongue.

It doesn't matter that I've always wanted to bang

in the dark, for everyone to see me, a flare
of brown eyes searching the black all around
for signs of my body. Sometimes it scares
the trees, the insects battling the grass, bound
by the blades like my body. I don't remember
how the cuts feel anymore or how a pair

of fat white thighs blinking in the moonlight
busted all the lamplight in the room. And now
we're in a room? Listen. Please touch my
body. That's all I wanted to say. Grab the clouds
down from the sky and free them. I know
my breasts feel in a lovely way like snow,

like their own flashing bulbs. I no longer like
that the sky can hear me, that the wind can break
my mind down to pieces. What I mean is a lie.
What I mean is new. What I mean is so naked
I can't even open my fat mouth to breathe.
Touch me. Turn me to the stars that won't leave.

FAT GIRL LACHARTA

Reader, I know you don't know why
       the moon calls out to me to say
You go girl, but I love the way
       she says it, like it's fine I weigh
the most I've ever weighed. One time
       I called back, remembered the fine

I paid to that creepy cop, back
       when he pulled me over, the crack
of his grin, and how, then, he licked
       his mustache, my car window blacked-
out. I rolled it down and he looked
       away. He looked away. He booked

my body, not seeing my face
       until the sky turned over, laced
with light and then I watched him grace
       my body with his eyes, the price
of fatness. But the moon says *hey*
       each night. She opens up. She stays.

FAT GIRL TRIUMPHAL ODE

I'm not your pizza-stuffing
lard ass, not your slight
chance of gaining three pounds from that
accidental crouton in your salad. I'm a pressure
system moving
through a stomach, the sudden
gust wrecking a dumbbell
into mush. I move haloed
and chill, my body a masterpiece, two thighs
muggy as summer, my ass super-
saturated with sunlight screaming, *Look
at me*. Embrace the bulk
of my breasts, nipples like the *oh*
your open mouth makes, pink
as a cyclone on a weather map. I'm a pill
popper with a forecast
of weight gain. Give me my fucking
seat-belt extender. Take my dark eyes blotting

a white sheet. Bitch, I can jog

      a block after hitting the blunt. I can rock

      the turbulence of my sleeveless arms

better than a plane dipping

      in the wind. I'm not a rainbow, yet I swallow

my antidepressants with the same

      kind of grace. You, too, have such a pretty face.

FAT GIRL MINUTE

Someone: understand me! My mind
       frays on the mend
              like the pillow
     my mother sewed

then re-sewed once the stitches blew
       apart and flew
              missing. I mean
     fat girl, this dream

will pass, the one where no one takes
       your body, licks
              your lips for you,
     undoes your blue.

FAT GIRL CROWN

And then I wake to find my face on fire,

                    my body lit, my hands burning my bed,

which smells like cinder, ashes. I'm a liar

                    if I pretend I didn't wish it so. Instead,

let's take a moment, pause to get it right:

                    I wake to find my face on fire, baked.

My body fat, my body still so bright

                    when the fire spins the room into a lake

of red-kissed hair and scraps of red-flecked skin

                    that keep on burning when I make no sound

aside from breathing out and breathing in

                    the smoke. But I could never figure out

just how the fire started or how I'd catch

                    the one who turned my face into a match.

The one who turned my face into a match

                        wakes up beside me on the blazing threads

of blankets. I reach out to touch him, stretch

                        my body, fat and growing. I trace his head

and move so close my mouth brushes his lips.

                        He looks a little sweet I think and smiles

without seeming to notice that these slits

                        of light still scorch across the carpet. Tiles

shatter along the bathroom floor. The walls

                        boil, and paint peels down like skin. It lands

on my fat thighs, searing my dress. He falls

                        asleep beside me, hair parted in my hands.

I want to wake him up to tell him why

                        I need to thank him now for setting the fire.

I need to thank him now for setting the fire

        because the room erupted, a volcano,

where lava soaked the carpet and a pair

        of jeans that wouldn't fit. Then a tornado

whirled the embers around my burning lips.

        I touched them with my fingertips. I touched

the wind, my hands dissolved of fingerprints.

        I touched the man again who wouldn't budge,

who didn't see the ceiling change to blue,

        a blue the color of a pool, a robin's egg

or how my face cooled off and how it threw

        the room into an ice cube. I start to beg

the man to open his eyes, to look around

        but he keeps them squinted shut until I drown.

He keeps them squinted shut until I drown,

        the waves folding me under while I breathe

the water—effervescent—all around,

        but then the room dries up. I feel his teeth

on mine, a kiss that brings me back, a star

        shooting across my tongue. I hear him groan.

He watches me as if he wants to char

        my skull, to burn my body fat, my bones

into a pyre. I sit up to suck the air.

        He stares a moment, smiles sweet again

but still cries out when I pull back my hair,

        my face a fatter face. And then the rain

pours down against my body, my blotched skin.

        The man in bed beside me says my name.

The man in bed beside me says my name.

                        I don't remember who I am. My face

allows itself a breath, inhales the flames

                    dancing along my legs, and then the hiss

of wood. It splinters, stabs the walls. I spin

                    my hair within the blaze until it glows.

The man stands up and wears a crooked grin.

                    His face changes, contorts until I know

I've seen him somewhere prowling in the past.

                    Before I run away, he strokes my hair.

And then he grabs my waist. He doesn't ask

                    to touch me, fingers moving everywhere.

I try to suck my stomach in. It matters:

                    the arms around me feel me getting fatter.

The arms around me feel me getting fatter

                           so I close my eyes and listen to the sound

of paper curling, the fire eating letters

                           I wrote, the books I never read. His hands

roam up and down until the fire simmers,

                           boils the water steaming along the walls.

He drops his arms, watches the ceiling shimmer

                           as fire floats above us, destroying the gills

of fish that flicker within the sudden waves.

                           I remember him, I think, the moment I see

the way he watches when the stitches give

                           on my dress and the way he checks the seams

close up, so I inspect his face, his lips.

                           I press my icy tongue against them, lick.

I press my icy tongue against them, lick

          the sneer right off. I throw my fat hands up

and let them fall. The ocean water breaks

          and creeps along to where the light erupts.

Then his mouth comes after me. This time

          embers shoot from my fingers like the moon

unleashing sparks. They turn his smile grim.

          Light disappears when nighttime kills the room

into a shadow that bends the ceiling black.

          I no longer see his face, don't miss the way

he watched me die in bed but brought me back

          when my fat body never had a say

in how this dream would end, in my desire.

          And then I wake to find my face on fire.

FAT GIRL NONET

Come after me now. Let's lie in bed,

the room a frosted mug, the room

a wick sparked to fire. Pick.

Let me name you mugger

of beehives, name you

the sting between

my fat thighs,

parted

eyes.

FAT GIRL MADRIGAL

If only things were different I'd believe

in all the things you say about my body

like how it moves you when I move. I'm ready

to understand myself through you. Don't leave.

I'll learn my way around until I'm steady.

If only things were different I'd believe

in all the things you say about my body

like how my body curves and how it needs

your mouth and hands, your face awake and buried

in my hair. My love, I know you think I'm pretty

and if only things were different I'd believe

in all the things you say about my body

like how it moves you when I move. I'm ready.

NOTES

Invented Forms from *Shadow Poetry* (www.shadowpoetry.com)

Alouette: Jan Turner

Cascade: Udit Bhatia

Duo-rhyme: Mary L. Ports

Duplex: Jericho Brown

LaCharta: Laura Lamarca

La'Tuin: Laura Lamarca

Memento: Emily Romano

Monchielle: Jim T. Henriksen

Monotetra: Michael Walker

Paradelle: Billy Collins

Trilonnet: Shelley A. Cephas

Villonnet: D. Allen Jenkins

For information about additional forms in this book, please see Lewis Putnam Turco's invaluable resource, *The Book of Forms: A Handbook of Poetics, Including Odd and Invented Forms;* University Press of New England, 2012.

STEPHANIE ROGERS is the author of the poetry collections *Plucking the Stinger* and *Fat Girl Forms*, both published by Saturnalia Books. She grew up in Middletown, Ohio, the same steel town portrayed in the book and Netflix drama, *Hillbilly Elegy.* She was educated at The Ohio State University and the University of Cincinnati, and her work has appeared or is forthcoming in *Georgia Review, Ploughshares, Tin House, Poetry Northwest, Shenandoah, New Ohio Review,* and elsewhere. She lives outside of Nashville in Lebanon, TN.

Also by Stephanie Rogers:

Plucking the Stinger

Fat Girl Forms is printed in Adobe Caslon Pro.
www.saturnaliabooks.org